Searchlight BOOKS™

The Kids' Guide to Government

How the Legislative Branch Works

Zelda Wagner

Lerner Publications ◆ Minneapolis

Lerner Publications Company
An imprint of Lerner Publishing Group, Inc.
241 First Avenue North
Minneapolis, MN 55401 USA

For reading levels and more information, look up this title at www.lernerbooks.com.

Main body text set in Adrianna Regular.
Typeface provided by Chank.

Library of Congress Cataloging-in-Publication Data

Names: Wagner, Zelda, 2000– author.
Title: How the Legislative branch works / Zelda Wagner.
Description: Minneapolis, MN : Lerner Publications, [2025] | Series: Searchlight books. The kids' guide to government | Includes bibliographical references and index. | Audience: Ages 8–11 | Audience: Grades 4–6 | Summary: "Congress is made up of two parts: the Senate and the House of Representatives. From introducing bills to passing them, young readers will discover how the legislative branch works"—Provided by publisher.
Identifiers: LCCN 2023041976 (print) | LCCN 2023041977 (ebook) | ISBN 9798765626627 (library binding) | ISBN 9798765629635 (paperback) | ISBN 9798765637203 (epub)
Subjects: LCSH: United States. Congress—Juvenile literature. | Legislation—United States—Juvenile literature. | Separation of powers—United States—Juvenile literature. | Legislative power
Classification: LCC JK1021 .W33 2025 (print) | LCC JK1021 (ebook) | DDC 328.73—dc23/eng/20230914

LC record available at https://lccn.loc.gov/2023041976
LC ebook record available at https://lccn.loc.gov/2023041977

Manufactured in the United States of America
1-1009930-51993-11/13/2023

Table of Contents

Chapter 1

DUTIES OF THE LEGISLATIVE BRANCH

Bang! A gavel strikes a desk in the US Capitol in Washington, DC. Silence falls across the room. The room holds 435 members of the House of Representatives. On the other side of the building, another gavel strikes. It grabs the 100-member Senate's attention and brings their meeting to order.

Both groups make up the US Congress. Together, they share the important job of making laws for the country.

Inside the Capitol

Visitors can see inside both chambers. At first, the work of the legislature can seem quiet. Congressional members shuffle papers and huddle to speak privately. But sometimes members rise to debate, and excitement can fill the room during a vote. Members vote yes or no. This is what representative democracy looks like.

Members of the House of Representatives in 2022

Behind the Constitution

In the late eighteenth century, Americans fought in the Revolutionary War (1775–1783) against Great Britain. Americans wanted to elect their own Congress. Before the war, American colonists were under the laws of Parliament, Britain's government. American colonists could not send representatives to vote on laws made in Parliament. But they still had to obey Britain's laws. This experience inspired a group of colonists to write the US Constitution in 1787.

A painting showing the end of the Revolutionary War

LEADERS DURING THE SIGNING OF THE US CONSTITUTION

In the Constitution, the authors mentioned the powers of Congress first. The powers of the executive branch and judicial branch were mentioned later. The Constitution gave Congress the power to approve the president's choices for Supreme Court justices and the president's advisers.

People vote at election booths during an election year.

Voting Power

US citizens eighteen and older can vote. Voters elect members of the House of Representatives and Senate. These members of Congress work in Washington, DC. They make laws that affect the lives of everyone in the country. That's why voters must carefully consider the ideas and leadership skills of the people they elect.

Members of Congress must be US citizens who live in the state they represent. Representatives must be at least twenty-five years old. Senators must be at least thirty.

Democracy and You

You don't have to be eighteen to make a difference by voting. Anybody can reach out to Congress. With the help of a trusted grown-up, you can find out who your state senators and representatives are. You might have an opinion on a bill they're considering. You might be for or against it. Write a letter or email to them with your thoughts. Members of Congress care about the opinions of the people they represent. Often members will change their vote on something if the people they represent strongly agree or disagree.

Voters also elect members of their state legislatures. These are bodies of government that serve a state, not the country. State legislatures make laws that affect only the citizens of that state.

In 2019, voters elected Alexandria Ocasio-Cortez into Congress. She became the youngest woman ever to serve in the US House of Representatives. She was twenty-nine years old.

Alexandria Ocasio-Cortez (*third from left*) during her swearing-in ceremony

Chapter 2

AN INSIDE LOOK AT CONGRESS

When the Constitution was being written, state leaders worried about how much power they would have in Congress. States with many residents thought they should be allowed to send more people to Congress. But smaller states with fewer residents wanted an equal voice in Congress. Having two branches of Congress solved this problem.

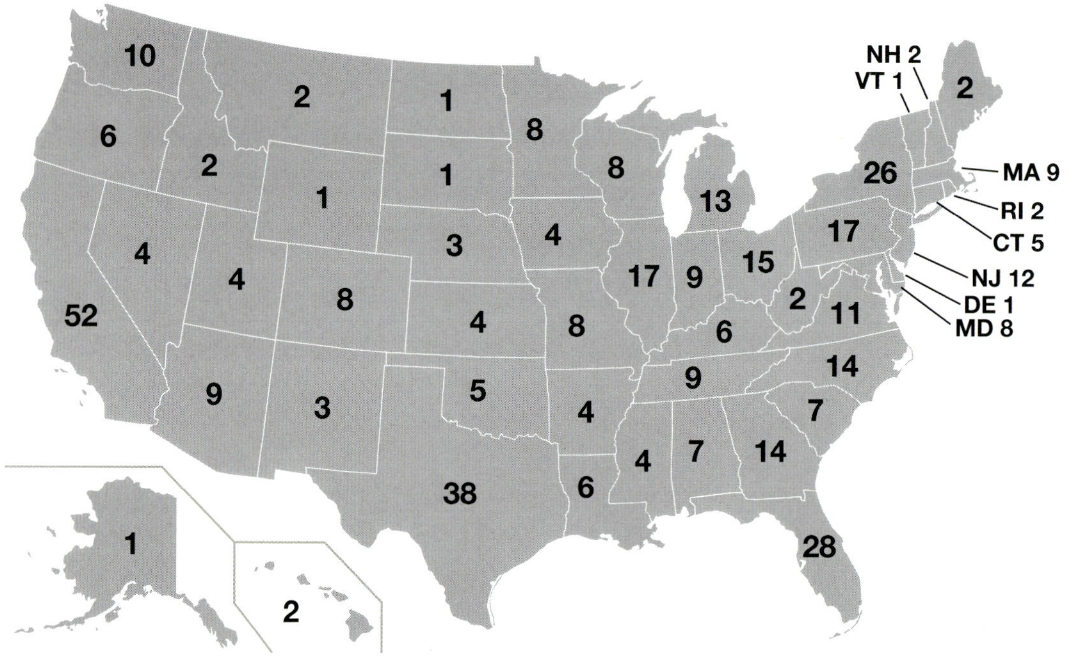

The number of House representatives from each state in 2020

Sharing Power

Having both a House of Representatives and a Senate made states of every population size happy. In the Senate, all states have equal power because each state elects two senators. The population of each state determines how many representatives each state sends to the House. California, for example, has fifty-two representatives. Wyoming has only one.

Two Busy Chambers

A raised platform in each chamber holds a desk for a leader. The Speaker of the House sits with a US flag draped behind the desk. A blue-and-gold curtain hangs behind the Senate leader's desk. The vice president of the United States presides over the Senate. But the vice president's only duty there is to break a vote when there's a tie.

The Speaker of the House can also call Congress to attention by hitting a gavel.

President Joe Biden giving his State of the Union address to Congress in 2023

Do you like to sit near your friends in class? Congress members like to sit with the same group every day too. In the House of Representatives, members of the Democratic Party fill the seats on the Speaker's right. Members of the Republican Party sit on the left. The desks in the Senate are organized in the same way. Aisles run down each chamber separating these groups.

Deep Dive

Some states and towns once passed unfair laws that forced Black people and white people to live separately. They could not sit together in movie theaters, in restaurants, or on buses. Black people and white supporters protested to show the country's leaders that this was unacceptable. They marched through cities and sat down together in public places. Police often arrested them. Congress finally passed a federal law in 1964 that made these unfair state laws illegal.

Different Views

Different ideas about the role of the government also divide these two groups. Democrats tend to believe the government should control the power of businesses and spend money to help citizens in need. Republicans tend to want a smaller federal government with fewer rules and regulations. Most debates in Congress occur between Democrats and Republicans.

Democrat Stacy Plaskett (*right*) debates with Republican Jim Jordan (*left*) during a congressional hearing.

Chapter 3

MAKING LAWS

The Capitol's dome rises between the House of Representatives and the Senate chambers. Formal events take place in the vast, round room below. Bills ready to be made into laws pass through here.

The US Capitol rotunda is open to visitors and connects the House and Senate chambers.

Sharing Duties

Both branches of Congress divide the work of making laws and important decisions. For example, all bills to raise money for the federal government must start in the House of Representatives. These bills become laws that tell citizens how much to pay in federal taxes. Similarly, only the Senate can approve treaties with other countries.

From Idea to Bill to Law

The two chambers work together to pass laws. US citizens can send ideas for new laws to the representatives or senators from their state. When an idea starts in the House, representatives discuss it with one another. If enough representatives support the idea, it is written as a bill. The same happens in the Senate. New bills can start in either the House or Senate.

House Republican members discuss a new bill.

In the House of Representatives, bills are placed in a wooden box, or hopper. Each bill is given a number. Members of the House discuss whether a bill should be passed. The Speaker of the House assigns the bill to a committee. Each member of the committee is an expert on a topic, such as agriculture, education, or health.

HOPPERS ARE PLACED NEXT TO THE CLERK'S DESK IN THE HOUSE OF REPRESENTATIVES.

Republican Garret Graves speaks to members of the House after a vote to approve a new energy cost bill.

Committee members study the bill, research the topic, and may even make changes to it. Then they present the bill to all members of the House for a vote. If a majority of representatives do not agree to pass the bill, it won't become a law. Most bills don't survive this vote.

A Few Winners

Successful bills go through both chambers of Congress. For example, if most representatives favor a bill, it travels to the Senate for approval. There, it passes through more committees, debates, and votes.

President Barack Obama signing a treaty in the White House

If most senators vote for the bill, it heads to the White House. There, the president can sign the bill to make it a law. The president can also veto, or reject, it. But the bill can still become law if two-thirds of all representatives and senators support it in a new vote. Or, if the president ignores the bill, after ten days with Congress in session, the bill becomes a law.

Thousands of bills are introduced each year in Congress. Yet only about 5 to 10 percent of those bills become laws. But members of Congress can still introduce bills to adjust these laws. The US Supreme Court can also strike down a law if the court decides it is unconstitutional.

Justices of the Supreme Court in 2022

Chapter 4

THE LEGISLATIVE BRANCH AND YOU

Strom Thurmond, a senator from South Carolina, holds the record for the longest filibuster in US history. A filibuster is an effort by a congressional member to delay or stop the passage of a bill, usually through a long speech. Thurmond spoke against the Civil Rights Act of 1957 for more than twenty-four hours.

Congressional members must consider what interests their voters. Voters in rural areas might be interested in how Congress votes on agricultural bills.

Voters living on the coast are probably interested in bills about controlling floods.

Keeping People Safe

Members of Congress know safety is important to everyone. Federal laws protect people in every part of daily life. Labels must warn us if cleaning products are poisonous. Labels must list food ingredients. And drinking water must be tested for dangerous chemicals. Congress has also passed laws to limit pollution in the air we breathe.

Congress passed the Cleaning Product Labeling Act in 2017.

Congress passed the Children's Online Privacy Protection Act in 1998 to protect children's privacy on the internet.

People especially want children to be safe. Congress does too. Federal laws require all products for children to be tested for safety. Schools must provide healthful meals to children. Congress has also passed laws to protect the privacy of internet users under thirteen years old.

Deep Dive

If you lived a century ago, you might have been working in a factory for up to eighteen hours a day. Instead of doing schoolwork, children often ran dangerous equipment and carried heavy loads. By 1900, half of the US states had passed laws that made child labor illegal. But Congress had to step in to pass a federal law that prevents children under the age of fourteen from working at most jobs.

People can write letters, vote, or protest to have their voices heard.

Vote for Change

If citizens are not happy with the work Congress has done, they can vote for new lawmakers. Citizens who are at least eighteen years old can vote for representatives every two years. Senators face elections every six years. Those under eighteen can make a difference too. If you have an idea that could make people's lives safer or easier, write to your representative and senator. Remember, the legislative branch represents you!

What Do You Think?

Should Congress pass a law to ban restaurants from serving sugary drinks to children? People have strong opinions on this issue. Some people believe that laws must protect children's health. Children can suffer from health problems from drinking too many sugary drinks. Other people believe that only parents can teach children to make healthful choices. They believe that a ban takes away a family's freedom to make its own rules.

What do you think? Should Congress decide what children can and cannot drink?

Glossary

chamber: a room or a division of a legislative body

citizen: a person who lives in a city, state, or country and is protected by its government

committee: a group of people chosen to discuss a particular issue and make decisions for a larger group

debate: a discussion in which people express different opinions

democracy: a form of government in which the people choose their leaders in elections

executive branch: the branch of US or state government that carries out laws

federal: relating to the laws made and enforced by the central or national government

gavel: a small wooden hammer that is used to signal the beginning of a meeting or to call for quiet

judicial branch: the branch of government that interprets and applies laws and decides if they follow the Constitution

legislature: a group of people who have the power to make or change laws for a country or state

veto: to stop a bill from becoming a law

Learn More

Ben's Guide: The Legislative Branch
https://bensguide.gpo.gov/a-legislative

Kiddle: Federal Government of the United States Facts for Kids
https://kids.kiddle.co/Federal_government_of_the_United_States

Kids in the House
https://kids-clerk.house.gov/grade-school/

Stratton, Connor. *Congress*. Lake Elmo, MN: Focus Readers, 2024.

Tyner, Dr. Artika R. *Black Achievements in Politics: Celebrating Shirley Chisholm, Barack Obama, and More*. Minneapolis: Lerner Publications, 2024.

Winn, Kevin. *How Are Laws Made?* Ann Arbor, MI: Cherry Lake, 2023.

Index

Photo Acknowledgments

Image credits: AP Photo/Graeme Sloan/Sipa USA, p. 5; IanDagnall Computing/Alamy, p. 6; Ian Dagnall/Alamy, p. 7; adamkaz/Getty Images, p. 8; SAUL LOEB/Getty Images, p. 10; United States Census 2020, modified by Fredddie/Wikipedia, p. 12 (public domain); Jonathan Newton /The Washington Post/Getty Images, p. 13; ANDREW CABALLERO-REYNOLDS/AFP/Getty Images, p. 14; Alex Wong/Getty Images, pp. 16, 21; JIM WATSON/AFP/Getty Images, p. 18; Tom Williams/CQ-Roll Call, Inc/Getty Images, p. 19; Dennis Brack/Alamy, p. 20; MediaPunch Inc/Alamy, p. 22; OLIVIER DOULIERY/AFP/Getty Images, p. 23; Ute Grabowsky/Photothek/ Getty Images, p. 25; JGI/Jamie Grill/Getty Images, p. 26; SOPA Images/Getty Images, p. 28.

Cover: Chip Somodevilla/Getty Images.